A NEW APPROACH
TO SIGHT SINGING
REVISED EDITION

A NEW APPROACH
TO SIGHT SINGING
REVISED EDITION

SOL BERKOWITZ
PROFESSOR OF MUSIC

GABRIEL FONTRIER
PROFESSOR OF MUSIC

LEO KRAFT
PROFESSOR OF MUSIC

Queens College
of the City University
of New York

W · W · NORTON & COMPANY

New York · London

W. W. Norton & Company, Inc., 500 Fifth Avenue, New York, N.Y. 10110
W. W. Norton & Company Ltd., 25 New Street Square, London EC4A 3NT

Published simultaneously in Canada by Stoddart,
a subsidiary of General Publishing Co. Ltd,
Don Mills, Ontario.

Library of Congress Cataloging in Publication Data

Berkowitz, Sol.
A new approach to sight singing.

1.   Sight-singing.   I.   Fontrier, Gabriel, joint
author.   II.   Kraft, Leo, joint author.   II.   Title.
MT870.B485N5   1976   784.9′4   75–31660

Printed in the United States of America

0

ISBN 0-393-09194-5

To John Castellini,
our teacher, our good friend and colleague, our editor,
this book is affectionately dedicated.

CONTENTS

ACKNOWLEDGMENTS

It is a pleasure to acknowledge the wholehearted help and encouragement given to us, during the period in which this book was written, by our colleagues in the Queens College Music Department. Their suggestions were most stimulating and useful.

We are especially indebted to Professor John Castellini, our patient and devoted editor, who continually labored with our manuscript and helped define its final form. We gratefully thank Professor Saul Novack of the Music Department for his constructive help and advice, and Dr. Joseph Raben of the English Department for his careful reading of the prose in this book.

Many of our basic ideas concerning music and music theory were gained during our years as students and colleagues of the late Karol Rathaus. To him, then, we owe a special debt of gratitude.

And, since this book grew out of our classroom experience, we sincerely thank the many gifted and industrious students in our classes whose eagerness to learn led us to better understanding of what might prove most useful in *A New Approach to Sight Singing*.

Sol Berkowitz
Gabriel Fontrier
Leo Kraft

Queens College
January, 1960

PREFACE

This book consists of a coordinated body of musical material *specifically composed* for the study of sight singing. A mastery of the art of singing at sight is essential to the instrumentalist, the singer, the musicologist, indeed to any musician or intelligent amateur. Ideally, the young student should be taught this skill from the moment his vocal or instrumental instruction begins, but actually very few music students enjoy the benefits of such early training. Far too many reach an advanced level of instruction with little ability in sight singing, and this is often true even of students whose instrumental or vocal equipment is of professional concert caliber. Courses in sight singing, therefore, are a necessary part of the music curriculum of secondary schools, conservatories, colleges, and universities.

A number of textbooks have been published for use in sight-singing courses, which make use of excerpts from vocal and instrumental literature. The present volume, however, consists entirely of music especially composed for the study of sight singing. In more than a decade of teaching sight singing at Queens College of the City University of New York, the authors have written a considerable number of melodies and duets for classroom use. They found that they were able to strike a particular level of difficulty and focus upon specific problems more effectively by composing material to meet the students' needs than by using melodies drawn from standard literature. They have also tried to aid their students by devising exercises which could be practiced without the assistance of an instructor. This book includes drills of the type which have proved most useful. Thus, the entire book has grown out of classroom experience which has convinced the authors that material for the study of sight singing should be written especially for that purpose.

A New Approach to Sight Singing contains five chapters, supplementary exercises, and two appendixes. The first chapter contains melodies; the second, sets of variations; the third, duets; the fourth, accompanied melodies; the fifth, studies in melodic improvisation. The supplementary exercises consist of special drills which give added emphasis to the major/minor relationship, medieval Church modes, whole tone and chromatic scales, and advanced chromatic and atonal melodies. Appendix I contains a glossary of musical terms. Appendix II contains explanations of some musical signs.

Each chapter is divided into four sections, and the material in each section is graded in order of increasing difficulty. In every chapter, Section I consists of elementary material, Section II, intermediate, Sections III and IV, advanced. The unit of work is the section: Section I materials in each of the five chapters make up a coordinated body of music, and are intended to be used concurrently. The same applies to Sections II, III, and IV.

For example, students on the elementary level will begin with the first section of each of the chapters. A typical class hour might start with the singing of a group of melodies (Chapter One, Section I). One of the sets of variations (Chapter Two, Section I) might follow; the class could then turn to the duets (Chapter Three, Section I), the accompanied melodies (Chapter Four, Section I), or the improvisation studies (Chapter Five, Section I). It is not expected that all five chapters will be drawn upon in the course of any one hour. The bulk of class time will probably be devoted to the melodies, which comprise about one half of the book. But the frequent use of Chapters Two, Three, Four, and Five will make possible a variety of approaches to the study of sight singing, and will also show the student how the skill which he acquires in any one area can be extended and applied to other musical situations.

A New Approach to Sight Singing is so organized that it may be adapted to various programs of study. Sections I and II, being essentially diatonic, may be integrated with the study of diatonic harmony, while Sections III and IV lend themselves to coordination with the study of chromatic harmony and atonality.

The *Melodies,* which constitute Chapter One, encompass a wide variety of musical styles and are graded progressively in terms of both technical and musical difficulty.

Section I, consisting of diatonic melodies, emphasizes the fundamental aspects of tonality. Stepwise motion, skips in simple contexts, and basic rhythmic patterns serve to introduce elementary problems of sight singing.

The melodies of Section II, while still diatonic, include simple modulations to the dominant or relative major, and gradually introduce more difficult rhythms.

Section III contains melodies with more elaborate modulations and chromatic embellishments, and introduces modal idioms. Phrase structures are more diverse, rhythms more complex.

In Section IV, atonal melodies are introduced and the exercises include more challenging problems in tonality, rhythm and meter, phrase structure, dynamics, and musical interpretation.

The treble, alto, and bass clefs are used in all sections; the tenor clef is introduced in Section IV.

From one melody to the next the student will encounter some changes of key, clef, rhythm, meter, tempo, dynamics, phrasing, and style. Grouping the melodies according to isolated technical characteristics has been deliberately avoided, for such an approach is arbitrary and unmusical. Rather, a more realistic approach is followed whereby the student is gradually introduced to the manifold problems he will face in practical musical situations. Moreover, within each level of difficulty there is a diversity of musical styles as well as technical problems. Some melodies embody the expansive contour of the Baroque line; some demonstrate nineteenth-century chromaticism; others derive from folk and jazz idioms.

The *Themes and Variations,* Chapter Two, provide the experience of singing compositions of relatively extended duration, and also emphasize problems of musical interpretation. Because the character of the melodies changes from one variation to another, the student is helped to develop a sensitive performance technique.

Chapters Three, Four, and Five serve a twofold purpose. First, they stimulate the study of sight singing by approaching it from different points of view. Second, they present many different musical problems whose solutions demand applications of varied sight singing techniques.

The *Duets*, Chapter Three, have as their purpose the development of independence, as well as a sense of ensemble in part singing.

Chapter Four, which introduces the use of the piano, will help the student to increase his awareness of correct intonation. This chapter also encourages the discipline of a steady rhythm, and develops coordination between singing and playing. These *Play and Sing* exercises also point up the harmonic implications of a melodic line.

The *Improvisation Studies*, which comprise Chapter Five, add a new dimension to the study of sight singing. These studies are designed to help develop a good understanding of the relationship among melody, harmony, and rhythm. They require the student to look ahead, to "sight" before he sings, and to start thinking in terms of a complete musical phrase.

The *Supplementary Exercises* provide a variety of materials designed as drills in intervalic relationships, intonation, and rhythm. Part One of the *Supplementary Exercises* is designed for use with Sections I and II of the five chapters, while Part Two is to be used with Sections III and IV.

Everyone can learn to sing. Whether or not he possesses a beautiful voice, anyone can achieve satisfactory sight singing ability by consistent study. Correct sight singing is a skill, a developed ability, and can be acquired through diligent practice. The satisfaction gained in developing such an important skill will more than justify the hours devoted to the study of this discipline. Sight singing is certainly not an end in itself, but only one of many necessary skills which any intelligent musician must develop. Music does not live on paper. To bring it to life there must be an instrument that can sing, an ear that can hear, and a sensitive mind that can sing and hear in the silence of thought.

Preface to the Revised Edition

A dozen additional years of experience have led to a number of revisions in this text. The basic format, however, has proved itself in the classroom and remains unchanged. While every teacher may not use every chapter, different instructors use different combinations of chapters. For this reason we have retained all the types of exercises in the second edition.

In general, those exercises which had proven least useful in teaching were replaced. Beyond that, others were rewritten to heighten their effectiveness. New material was composed for all levels; in particular, twentieth-century idioms are now to be found in considerably greater number.

Chapter One, *Melodies*, has been strengthened and increased from 499 exercises to 576. A group of modal melodies is now to be found at the end of Section II, for quick reference.

Chapter Two, *Themes and Variations*, has been revised and expanded.

Chapter Three, *Duets*, has been considerably amplified. A group of modal duets now concludes Section II, paralleling the modal melodies.

Chapter Four, *Play and Sing*, has also been enlarged. Additional exercises in Section I, in particular, give the student increased opportunity to study melody in the context of basic harmonic progressions. In this chapter, too, new material deals with the styles of the recent past.

We wish to thank our many colleagues who have used this book during the last decade for their many constructive suggestions.

It is our hope that the enlarged scope of this edition will increase its usefulness to the many young people who strive to master the basic skills of music.

Sol Berkowitz
Gabriel Fontrier
Leo Kraft

Queens College
May, 1975

A NEW APPROACH
TO SIGHT SINGING
REVISED EDITION

CHAPTER ONE
MELODIES

Before singing a melody (or performing music of any sort) it is necessary to understand thoroughly the system of music notation we use today. The five-line staff with the clef signs, time signatures, tempo indications, and expression markings constitute a music code, all the elements of which must be decoded simultaneously in order to transform into meaningful music what has been set down on paper.

ESTABLISH THE KEY

The melodies in Section I are tonal. Each is written in a specific key and the student must establish that key before attempting to sing. The tonic note of the key (rather than the first note of the melody) should be played on the piano or the pitch pipe and sung by the student. Then the scale of the key should be sung, ascending and descending, after which an arpeggio consisting of tonic, third, fifth, and octave may be sung to establish further a feeling for the tonality of the melody.

ESTABLISH THE TEMPO

Next it is necessary to take cognizance of the tempo (rate of speed) and the meter (number of beats to the measure). Many different tempo indications have been used in this book to familiarize the student with most of the terms in common use. It is important that the singer know the meaning of these tempo markings, all of which are to be found in the Glossary (page 358).

The time signature denotes meter. Simple meters (duple, triple, and quadruple) are indicated by signatures having a 2, 3, or 4 as the upper numeral, or by the signs C (corresponding to $\frac{4}{4}$ meter) or $\mathvarphi$ (*alla breve*, corresponding to $\frac{2}{2}$ meter). Regular compounded meters ($\frac{6}{8}$, $\frac{9}{8}$, and $\frac{12}{8}$) are combinations of simple meters within one measure.

Tempo can be established and meter defined by the student if he beats time as a conductor does. Standard conducting patterns should be used consistently. $\frac{6}{8}$ time may be conducted in six or in two beats; $\frac{9}{8}$ and $\frac{12}{8}$ time in separate beats or in three or four beats respectively. Tempo, and often the character of a melody, will serve the student in determining how to conduct compound meters.

1

SINGING MELODIES WITHOUT TEXTS

It is advisable to sing some definite syllable for every note the better to control quality and intonation. In many foreign countries *solfeggio* (the application of the *sol-fa* syllables to the degrees of the scale) is used in sight singing. This practice is officially sanctioned by foreign national conservatories. In our country, however, several methods of singing melodies without texts are in common use. These may be summarized as follows:

Fixed Do

In the fixed *Do* system, our notes, C, D, E, F, G, A, and B, are called *Do, Re, Mi, Fa, Sol, La,* and *Ti*. In singing a melody, the name for each note is sung without regard to any accidental. Countries which use this technique have been quite successful with it, perhaps because of the rigorous early training which their students receive.

Movable Do

In the movable *Do* system, *Do* always represents the tonic or first degree of the scale, regardless of key. Accidentals are accounted for by changing the syllables. The ascending chromatic scale reads as follows:

Do, Di, Re, Ri, Mi, Fa, Fi, Sol, Si, La, Li, Ti, Do

The descending chromatic scale reads as follows:

Do, Ti, Te, La, Le, Sol, Se, Fa, Mi, Me, Re, Ra, Do

When a melody modulates, the new tonic is called *Do*, and the other notes of the scale are renamed accordingly. The purpose of this system is to emphasize the relationship between the degrees of the scale, and to develop a feeling for tonality even when the tonal center shifts.

Other Methods

Numbers (1, 2, 3) may be used instead of syllables (*Do, Re, Mi*). The application is the same as in the movable *Do* system, except that there is no numeral change for the chromatic tones.

One syllable, such as *la*, may be used for all pitches. Thus the singer does not have to translate the pitch names into syllables or numbers.

A musician is expected to know the system in common use wherever he may be; therefore, the student should master more than one of these techniques.

PHRASING

The student is urged to avoid note-to-note singing and to make a genuine effort to grasp an entire phrase as a musical unit. To guide and encourage this process of looking ahead, slurs have been placed over the phrases of every melody. These slurs define the phrase structure and serve as a guide to breathing.

MUSICAL VALUES

In practicing the singing of melodies, as in practicing the piano or violin, the beginner may be tempted to concentrate his entire attention on producing the correct pitch, hoping that other musical values will be acquired in due course. But melodies do not exist without rhythm; they also have nuances of dynamics and tempo, and climaxes. These qualities are an integral part of the music. The student who wishes to improve his musicianship while learning the technique of sight singing must begin to think about musical values with the first melody in the book. As an aid to intelligent and sensitive performance we have included dynamics, expression, and articulation markings throughout the book. The eye should be trained to observe them; the mind to implement them.

Clearly, there is much to do, and it is suggested that the student *make haste slowly*. The first melodies should be studied carefully in order to develop good musical habits. The student should sing a melody several times, if necessary, until he can perform it with ease and fluency.

MELODIES *Section I*

SECTION I IS TO BE USED WITH SECTION I OF ALL OTHER CHAPTERS
(SEE PAGES 171, 208, 257, 319).

The first melodies emphasize the basic aspects of tonality. They were designed to include easily recognizable scale and chordal patterns. These diatonic melodies are based upon both major and minor modes.

The phrases are usually symmetrical and short enough to be grasped at a glance. However, the diversity of rhythms, keys, modes, tempos, dynamics, and clefs should provide a variety of musical experiences. The alto clef is introduced with #34; compound meter $\frac{6}{8}$ with #51; the minor mode with #89.

Students who are unfamiliar with one or another of the clefs that are used in this section should prepare for the actual singing by reciting the names of the notes in strict time. Then the melody should be sung, again naming the notes. To develop facility in reading the various clefs, the student should also *play* the melodies which have been sung in class.

1. Andante con moto

2. Andante

3. Andante

4. Allegro

5. Allegretto

6. Allegro

7. Moderato

8. Allegro deciso

9. Andantino

10. Andante con moto

11. Larghetto

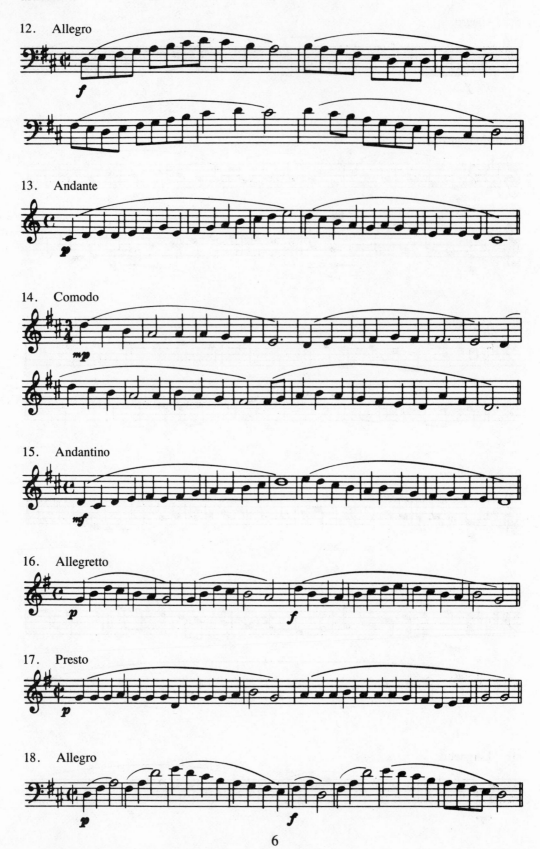

19. Allegretto

20. Andante

21. Vivace

22. Andante

23. Allegro

24. Andante

25. Allegro

26. Moderato

27. Andante con moto

28. Allegretto

29. Andante

30. Gaio

31. Allegro

32. Allegro

33. Andante sostenuto

The same melody written with three different clefs

34a. Moderato

34b. Moderato

34c. Moderato

35. Andante espressivo

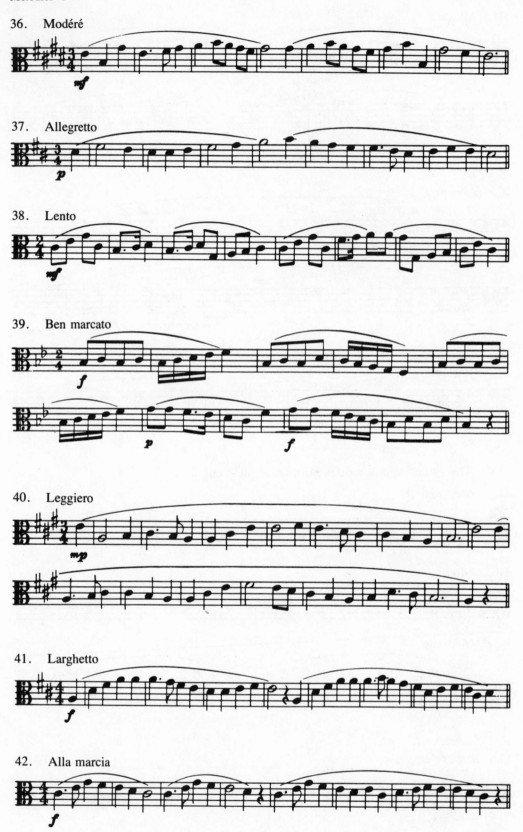

43. Con moto

44. Allegro

45. Allegro deciso

46. Allegro

47. Tempo di menuetto

48. Alla marcia

49. Moderato

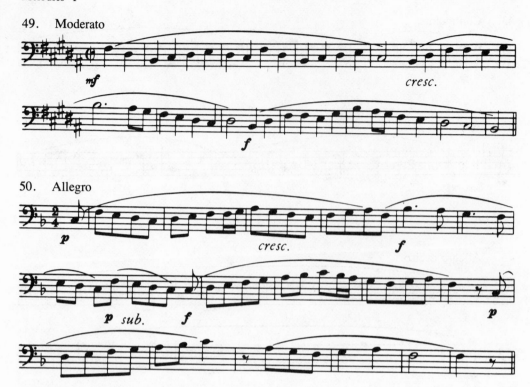

50. Allegro

The same melody notated in three different meters

51a.

51b.

51c.

52. Andante

58. Andante

59. Andante con moto

60. Allegro

61. Andante sostenuto

62. Andantino

63. Andantino

64. Allegro

65. Andante sostenuto

66. Con moto

67. Vivo

68. Andante

69. Valse

70. Moderato

71. Andante cantabile

72. Lentement

73. Allegro

74. Moderato

75. Allegro

76. Allegro

77. Sustained

83. Animato

84. Ben ritmico

85. Adagietto

86. Lively

87. Allegro

88. Allegro

Three C-minor scales

Natural

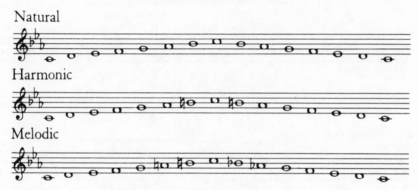

Harmonic

Melodic

For a set of exercises comparing the major and minor modes,
see *Supplement*, p. 337.

89. Moderato

90. En allant

91. Bewegt

92. Allegro

93. Comodo

94. Assez lent

95. Allegretto

96. Allegretto

97. Frisch und munter

98. Andante

99. Andantino

100. Andante

101. Langsam

102. Vif et léger

103. Andante con moto

104. Andantino marziale

105. Allegretto

106. Andante

107. Larghetto

108. Gigue

109. Valse

110. Andante e mesto

111. Andante

112. Grazioso

113. Lentement

114. Allegretto

115. Andante

125. Allegretto grazioso

126. Allegretto

127. Larghetto

128. Allegretto

129. Allegro

130. Andante con moto

131. Doux et expressif

132. Ländler

133. Nicht zu schnell

134. Con moto

135. Allegretto

136. Allegro Moderato (Var. V of *Themes and Variations,* 5, p. 177)

137. Mässig

138. Andante

139. Ziemlich schnell

140. Andante

141. Allegro

142. Assez vite

143. Lively

144. Brisk

MELODIES *Section II*

SECTION II IS TO BE USED WITH SECTION II OF ALL OTHER CHAPTERS
(SEE PAGES 180, 216, 263, 322).

These melodies contain simple modulations, more complex rhythms, and diatonic skips in a variety of contexts. As in Melodies, Section I, the tonality of each melody is clearly defined. Some phrases are longer; some less symmetrical; syncopations are introduced; and the vocal range is extended.

A group of modal melodies begins with #274.

148. Larghetto

149. Maestoso

150. Andante sostenuto

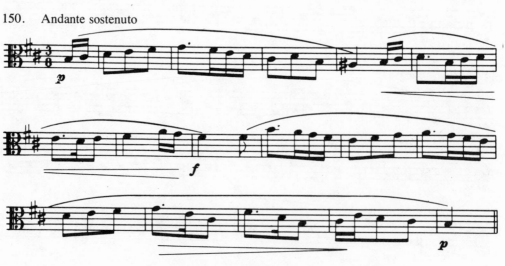

151. Allegretto

152. Con moto

153. Andante

154.   En allant

155.   Andante sostenuto

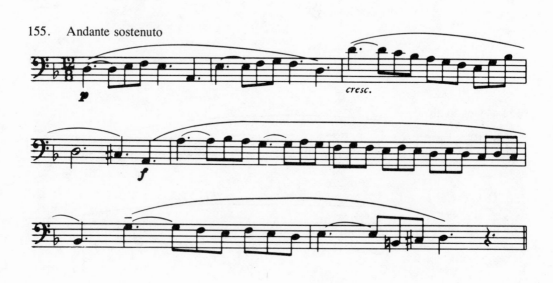

156.   Adagietto

157. Slowly

158. Con moto

159. Allegro grazioso

160. Comodo

161. Allegro

162. Etwas langsam

163. Andante pastorale

164. Andantino

169. Assez animé

170. Allegretto

171. ♩. = 60

172. Allegro

173. Valse

174. Allegro

175. Adagio

176. Zart

177. Moderato

FINE

DA CAPO AL FINE

178. Moderato

179. Lively

180. Pastorale

181. Ballando

182. Gai

183. Fliessend

184. Giocoso

185. Ländler

186. Allegro e ben marcato

187. Andante gioviale

188. Andantino

189. Allegro

190. Andante e mesto

191. Mässig

192. Gaily

193. Allegro

194. Allegro con brio

195. Andante espressivo

196. Allegretto (Var. V of *Themes and Variations*, 7, p. 181)

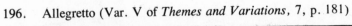

197. Andante

198. Moderato

199. Allegro

200. En allant

201. Mässig und zart

202. Fast, in one

203. Gaily

204. Doucement

205. Allegro moderato

206. Allegretto

207. Minuet

208. Andante espressivo

209. Andante

210. Andantino

211. Lilting

212. Ben ritmico

213. Maestoso

214. Animé

215. Moderato

decresc. poco a poco

216. Allegro grazioso

217. Ziemlich schnell

218. Allegretto

219. Lento (Melody of *Play and Sing*, 29, p. 265)

220. Allegro

221. Allegretto (Var. II of *Themes and Variations*, 10, p. 186)

222. Allegro moderato

FINE

più forte

p subito

D. C. AL FINE

223. Lively

224. Ziemlich langsam

225. Walzer

FINE

D. C. AL FINE

226. Allegro

227. Andante cantabile

228. Allegro

229. Pas trop vif

230. Fanfare

231. Andante sostenuto

232. Valse

233. Allegretto

234. Lento

235. Moderato

236. Fast

237. Modéré

238. Allegro gioviale

239. Briskly

240. Etwas gedehnt

241. Fast with a well-marked rhythm

242. Comodo

243. Minuet

Fine

D. C. al Fine

244. Largo e pesante

245. Andante

246. Mässig und ausdrucksvoll

247. Allegro

248. Ländler

249. Lively

250. Moderato

251. Allegretto

252. Adagio

257. Valse

258. Moderato

259. Medium bounce

268. Largo e mesto

269. Gigue

270. Larghetto

Modal Melodies Based on the Following Four Modes

Dorain

Phrygian

Mixolydian

Aeolian

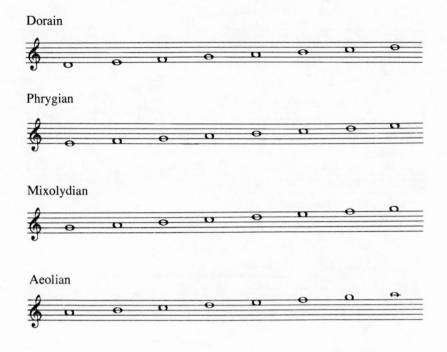

274.   Andante (Dorian)

275. Moderato (Dorian)

276. Andante (Transposed Dorian)

277. Largo (Phrygian)

278. Mesto (Phrygian)

279. Andante (Phrygian)

280. Adagietto (Mixolydian)

281. Moderato (Mixolydian)

282. Allegro (Mixolydian)

283. Lento (Aeolian)

284. Andante sostenuto (Transposed Aeolian)

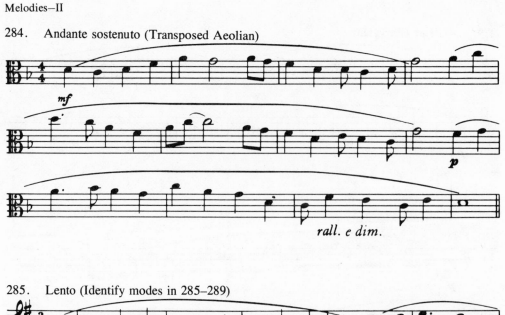

285. Lento (Identify modes in 285–289)

286. Gaio

287. Moving

288. Allegretto

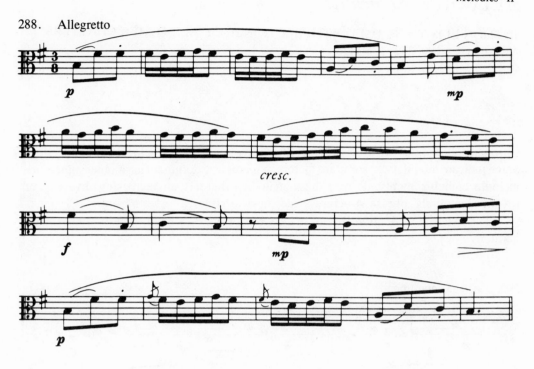

289. Fairly slow

MELODIES *Section III*

SECTION III IS TO BE USED WITH SECTION III OF ALL OTHER CHAPTERS (SEE PAGES 190, 230, 276, 326).

Chromatic alterations are used with increasing frequency in the melodies of this section. Some indicate modulation; some are factors in secondary dominant harmonies; others are melodic embellishments. Within these melodies there is an increasing diversity of rhythms, intervals, phrase structures, and musical styles.

The material of Section III can readily be correlated with the study of chromatic harmony.

290. Allegro non troppo

291. Mit Kraft

292. Allegro gioviale

293. Allegretto grazioso (Theme of *Themes and Variations*, 13, p. 192)

294. Larghetto

295. Allegretto

296. Andantino

301. Allegretto

302. Ländler

303. Well accented

304. Sostenuto

305. Andante espressivo

306. Nicht zu langsam

307. Andante

308. Allegretto

309. Lent et doux

310. Allegro

311. Schnell und fröhlich

312. So schnell wie möglich

313. Modéré et gracieux

314. Allegro con brio

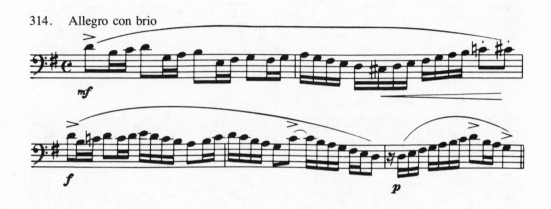

315. Ballando

316. Allegro

317. Allegro con spirito

318. Valse

319. Allegretto

320. Moderato

321.   Allegro moderato, alla ongarese

322.   Etwas langsam und zart

323.   Innig

324. Larghetto

325. Tempo di scherzo (in 1)

326. Briskly

327. Spiritoso

328. Tempo di minuetto

329. Ziemlich bewegt

330. Sehr rasch

331. Moderato

335. Allegro non troppo

336. Presto

337. Allegro giocoso

338. Lilting

339. Andantino

perdendosi

340. Lebhaft

341. Mässig, mit Empfindung

342. Tempo giusto

343. Allegretto

344. Allegro

345. Slowly and simply

346. Moderate

347. Moderate

348. Presto

349. Fast

353. Allegro moderato

354. Presto

355.   Andante semplice

356.   Medium bounce

357.   Animé et très expressif

358.   Allegretto

359.   Allegro

360.   Andante espressivo

361.   Vif et léger

362. **Rather slowly**

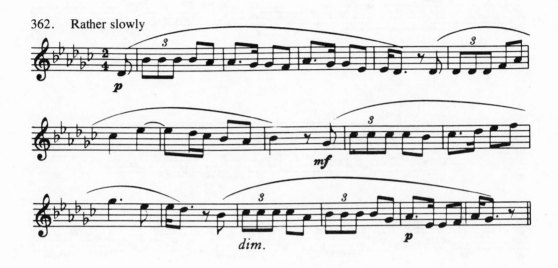

363. **Allegro e marcato**

364. **Waltz**

365. Mässig und einfach

366. Quasi presto

367. Modéré

368. Allegro giocoso

369. Allegretto

370. Saltarello

371. Adagio ed espressivo

372. Andante

373. Lively

374. Allegro

375. Moderato

376. Largo

377. Allegretto scherzoso

378. Freely

379. Allegro

380. Grave, con espressione

381. Allegretto

382. Langsam, mit Empfindung

383. Allegretto

384. Mazurka

385. Vif

386. Lebhaft

387. Ballando

388. Allegretto e leggiero

389. Galop

390. Lento assai

391. Lively

392. Il più presto possibile

393. Allegro

394. Alla marcia

395. Animated

396. Allegretto

397. Andante e rubato·

398. Allegro molto

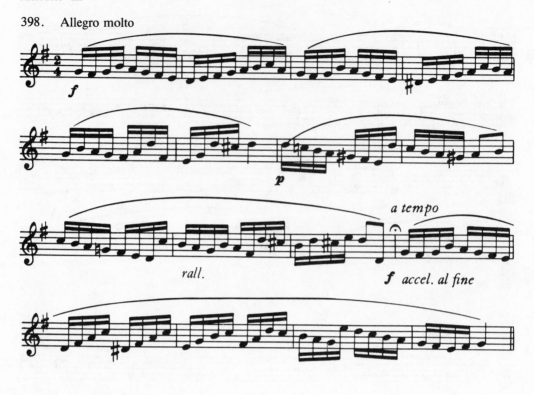

399. Moderato

400. Un poco sostenuto

401. Andante

402. Lively

403. Valse

404. Andantino

405. En allant

406. Vif et gai

407.   Etwas langsam und zart

408.   In jig time

409. Tempo di valse

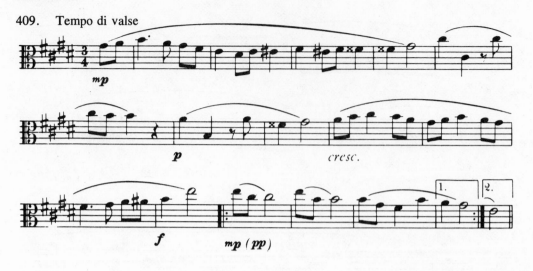

410. Adagio appassionato

411. Con calore

412. Allegro

413. Mässig und ausdrucksvoll

414. En allant

415. Adagio, senza rigore

416. Fast

417. Valse triste

418. Allegro non troppo

419. Bouncy

420. Andante, all'ongarese

421. Lento e mesto

422. Allegretto

MELODIES *Section IV*

SECTION IV IS TO BE USED WITH SECTION IV OF ALL OTHER CHAPTERS
(SEE PAGES 200, 242, 290, 330).

The melodies in this section present interesting problems of intonation, rhythm, and phrase structure. The tenor clef is introduced at the beginning of the section. Modulation to remote keys, the use of augmented and diminished intervals, a more intensified chromaticism, modal idioms, and complex syncopation offer the advanced student both challenge and stimulus.

    The concluding melodies of this section introduce 20th-century melodic idioms.

426. Andante

427. Allegro

428. Sostenuto

429. Presto

430. Allegro deciso

431. Allegretto

432. Vivace (Theme of *Themes and Variations*, 17, p. 200)

433. Lento

434. Mässig und ausdrucksvoll

435. Minuet

439. Lento

440. Con moto

441. Allegretto

442. Piacevole

443. Andantino

444. Lento

445. Valse brillante

446. Molto adagio

447. Andantino

448. Andante espressivo

449. Allegro

450. Langsam und ausdrucksvoll

451. Andante maestoso (Melody of *Play and Sing*, 70, p. 285)

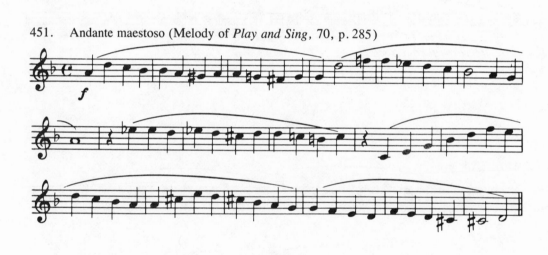

452. Adagio

453. Andante con moto

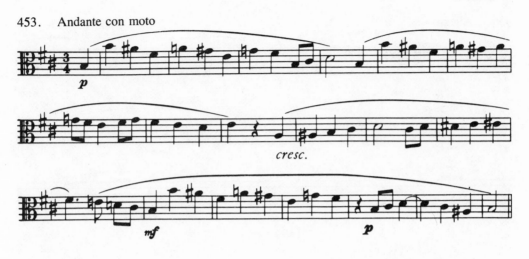

454. Andantino e leggiero

455. Freely

456. Allegro

457. March

458. Allegretto

459. Allegro energico

460. Allegro assai

461. Andante (Theme of *Themes and Variations*, 19, p. 204)

462. Con anima

463. Con calore

464. Mässig bewegt

465. Allegro

466. Andante

467. Con moto

468. Nicht zu schnell

469. Allegro

470. Langsam

471. Allegretto

472. Moderato e pomposo

473. Larghetto

474. Waltz

475. Free and easy

476. Ländler

477. Con calore

478. Allegretto

479. Andantino grazioso

480. Larghetto

481. Langsam

482. Andante con moto

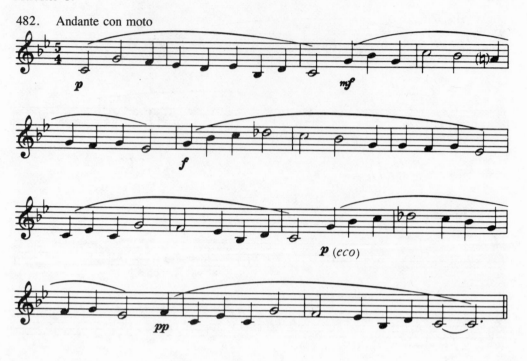

483. Ben ritmico

484. Allegretto

485. Waltz

FINE

DAL SEGNO AL FINE

486. Molto adagio e maestoso

487. Valse brillante

488. Moderato

489. Valse sentimentale

490. Lively

491. Etwas gedehnt

492. Allegro

493. Allegretto

494. Moderato

495. Arietta; andante

496. Andante cantabile

497. Mässig und stark

498. Andantino

499. Etwas langsam

zurückhalten

500. Briskly

501. Grave

142

502. Doux et lentement

503. Lento ed espressivo

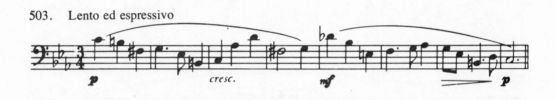

504. Allegro piacevole

505. Allegretto grazioso

506. Adagio

507. Andantino

508. Allegro energico

509. Tempo di valzer

510. Très vif et détaché

511. Adagietto

512. Allegretto

513. Allegretto

514. Valse triste

dim. al fine

rit.

515. Moderato e sostenuto

516. Andante e rubato

517. Allegro

518. Scherzo

519. Lebhaft und fröhlich

520. Allegro con brio

521. Mässig bewegt

522. Allegretto

523. Lento

524. Lento

decresc. e rit.

525. Allegro

a tempo

cresc.

f *p*

ritenuto

526. Lento

mf

poco rall.

527. Moderato e mesto

mf

cresc.

f

p

528. Largo espressivo

f

dim.

mp

cresc.

150

529. Tempo di Blues

530. Andante con moto

531. Allegro piacevole

532. Mazurka; moderato con anima

533. Slowly

534. Allegro

535. Avec movement

536. With a well-marked rhythm

537. Tempo di marcia

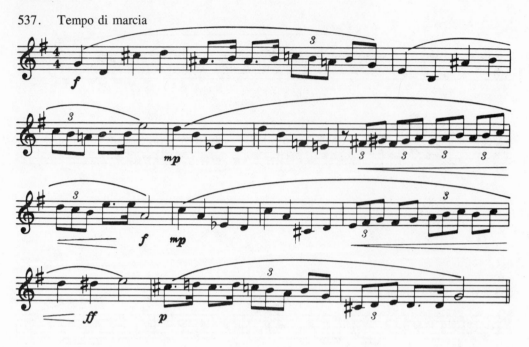

538. Allegro con spirito

539. Lento

540. Andante

541. Lento

542. Bewegt

543. Andante

544. With spirit

545. Lively

la seconda volta

546. Spiritoso

157

550. Tempo di minuetto

551. Allegro moderato

552. Allegro non tanto

553. Andante e semplice

554. Vivo

555. Vif

556. Expansively

557. Un poco pesante

558. Lebhaft und stark

559. Andantino

560. Mässig und zart

561. Allegro

562. Vivo

563. Andante espressivo

564. Allegro marcato

565. Andante e marcato

566. Allegro con moto

567. Allegro giocoso

568. Andante

569. Moderato

570. Piacevole

571. Pas trop vite, mais avec force

572. Allegro

573. Moderato

574. Mässig

165

575. Lento ed espressivo

576. Allegro giocoso

577. Gedehnt

578. Allegretto

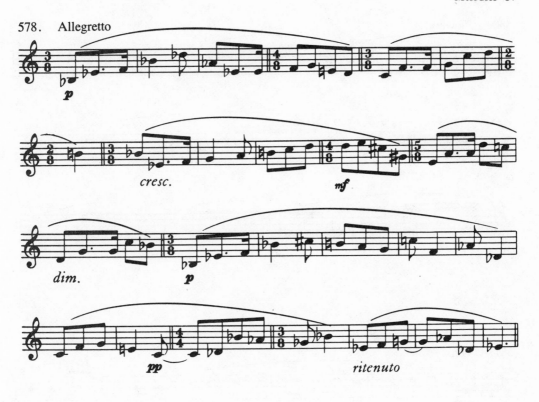

579. Ziemlich schnell

580. Flowing

581. Vivo

582. Allegretto

583. Moving

CHAPTER TWO
THEMES AND VARIATIONS
SECTIONS I, II, III, AND IV ARE TO BE USED WITH SECTIONS I, II, III, AND IV OF ALL OTHER CHAPTERS.

Themes and variations provide the opportunity of singing more extended musical compositions. The constantly changing character of the music as the variations unfold demands interpretive skills not required for the shorter melodies of Chapter One.

The nature of the material and the levels of difficulty are comparable to those of the melodies of Chapter One.

THEMES AND VARIATIONS *Section I*

Theme: Andante (Melody 3, p. 4)

Var. I: Andante

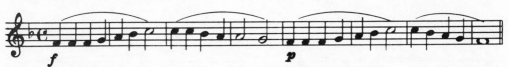

Var. II: Allegro

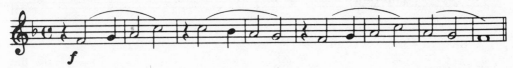

Var. III: Moderato

Var. IV: Lento

Var. V: Presto

cresc. poco a poco

Theme: Moderato

Var. I: Andante

Var. II: Allegro

Var. III: Presto

Var. IV: Lento

Var. V: Allegro con brio

THEME AND VARIATIONS, 3

Theme: Andante

p

Var. I: Andante

mp

Var. II: Andantino

mf

Var. III: Lento

f

Var. IV (Maggiore): Andante

Var. V: Allegretto

THEME AND VARIATIONS, 4

Theme: Larghetto

Var. I: L'istesso tempo

Var. II: Un poco allegro

Var. III: Allegretto

Var. IV (Minore): Lento

Var. V (Maggiore): Allegro molto

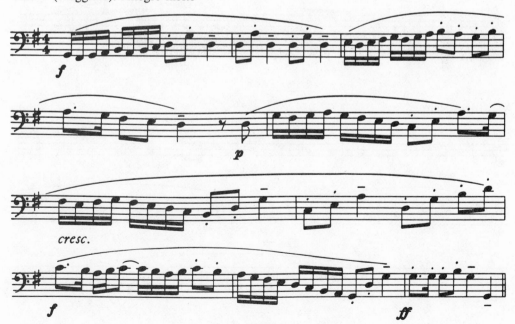

Theme: Allegro moderato

Var. I: Allegro

Var. II: Andantino

Var. III: Allegro

Var. IV: Tempo I

Var. V: Allegro con spirito

THEME AND VARIATIONS, 6

Theme: Moderato

Var. I: Moderato

Var. II: Poco più mosso

Var. III (Minore): Largo

Var. IV (Maggiore): Allegretto

Var. V: Allegro

THEMES AND VARIATIONS *Section II*

Theme: Allegro innocente

Var. I: Grazioso

Var. II: Andantino

Var. III: Andante

180

Var. IV (Minore): Adagietto

Var. V (Maggiore): Allegretto

THEME AND VARIATIONS, 8

Theme: Lento

Var. I: Un poco più mosso

Var. II: Andantino

Var. III: Allegretto

Var. IV (Maggiore): Adagio

Var. V (Minore): Allegro gioviale

Var. VI: Allegro

Theme: Moderato

Var. I: Moderato

Var. II: Allegretto

Var. III: Un poco sostenuto

Var. IV (Minore): Largo

Var. V (Maggiore): Allegro non troppo

THEME AND VARIATIONS, 10

Theme: Adagietto

Var. I: Alla marcia

185

Var. II: Allegretto

Var. III: Allegro misterioso

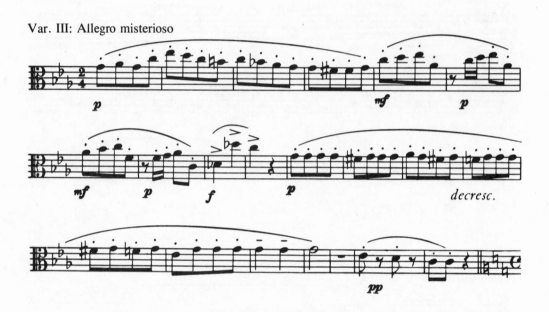

Var. IV (Maggiore): Largo e cantabile

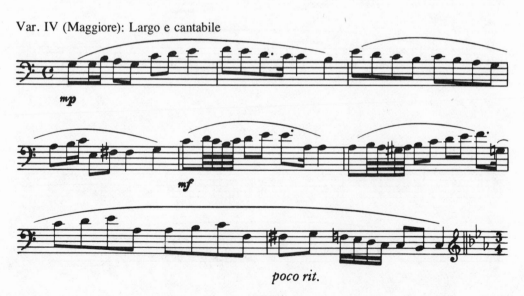

Var. V (Minore): Valse brillante

THEME AND VARIATIONS, 11

Theme: Allegretto gioviale

Var. I: Andantino

Var. II: Allegro ma non troppo

Var. III: Adagietto

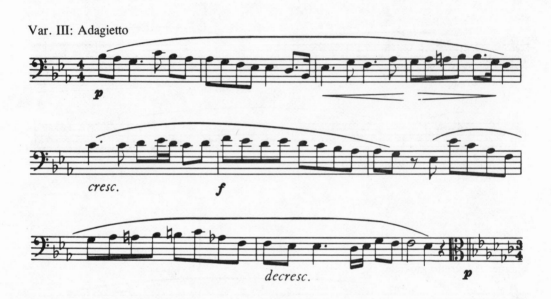

Var. IV (Minore): Un poco agitato

Var. V (Maggiore): Allegro con brio

THEMES AND VARIATIONS *Section III*

Theme: Allegro grazioso

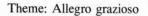

Var. I: Più allegro

Var. II: Un poco più mosso

Var. III (Minore): Moderato

Var. IV (Maggiore): Allegro con moto

Var. V: Tempo di valzer

Var. VI: Allegro

Theme: Allegretto grazioso

Var. I:

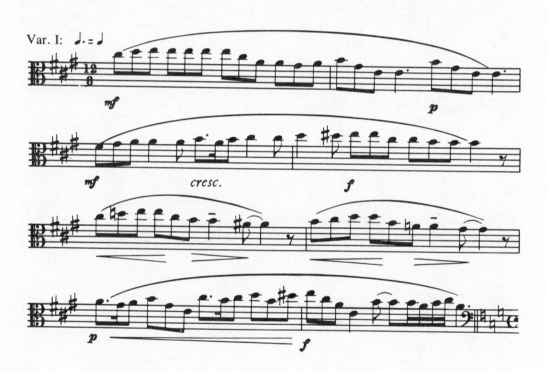

Var. II (Minore): Larghetto

Var. III (Maggiore): Adagietto

Var. IV: Allegro molto

Var. V: Allegro scherzando

THEME AND VARIATIONS, 14

Theme: Andante

Var. I: Andantino

Var. II: Allegro appassionato

sempre f

Var. III (Maggiore): Andante tranquillo

Var. IV (Minore): Allegretto

poco rit.

Var. V: Vivace

THEME AND VARIATIONS, 15*

Theme: Jolly

Var. I: Fast

*For review of Modes, see p. 69.

Var. II: Slowly

Var. III: Lively

Theme: Moderato

Var. I: Un poco meno mosso

Var. II: Allegro

poco rall.

THEMES AND VARIATIONS *Section IV*

Theme: Vivace

Var. I: Allegretto

Var. II (Minore): Moderate

Var. III: Un poco sostenuto

Var. IV (Maggiore): Allegro

Theme: Allegretto

Var. I: Andante

Var. II: Grazioso

Var. III (Minore): Allegro

Var. IV (Maggiore): Andantino cantabile

Var. V: Moderato

Var. VI: Allegro

THEME AND VARIATIONS, 19

Theme: Andante

Var. I:

Var. II (Maggiore): Un poco meno mosso

Var. III (Minore): Moderato

Var. IV: Allegro

Theme: Allegro deciso

Var. I: Allegretto

Var. II: Allegro

Var. III (Minore): Moderato

Var. IV: Presto

CHAPTER THREE
DUETS

SECTIONS I, II, III, AND IV ARE TO BE USED WITH SECTIONS I, II, III, AND IV OF ALL OTHER CHAPTERS.

The experience of singing one part while hearing another develops that sense of independence so essential to a good ensemble performer. His efforts to hear the harmonic and contrapuntal relation of his own melodic line to the other will guide the student toward maintaining correct intonation and rhythmic precision. For solo practice, it is useful to play one part at the piano while singing the other.

DUETS *Section I*

1. Allegretto

5. Allegretto

6. Allegro moderato

7. Allegretto

8. Andantino

9. Un poco sostenuto

10. Andante con moto

11. Moderato con moto

12. Allegretto

13. Minuetto

14. Andantino

15. Andante espressivo

16. Andantino

17. Allegro con spirito

18. Allegro

19. Allegretto

20. Allegro moderato

21. Allegretto

22. Allegro

DUETS *Section II*

23. Giocoso

24. Andante espressivo

25. Mässig

26. Lento

27. Giocoso

28. En allant

29. Andantino

30. Andantino

31. Allegretto giocoso

32. Andante cantabile

33. Moderato

34. Mässig

35. Moderato

36. Allegro gioviale

37. Moderato ed espressivo

38. Andantino

39. Un poco sostenuto

40. Allegro

41. Lively

42. Tempo di minuetto

43. Andantino

44. Allegro non troppo

45. Allegro con spirito

46. Allegretto

47. Con brio

48. Andantino

49. Andantino

50. Ben ritmico

51. Moderately slow

52.   Moderately fast

53.   Modéré

54. Andante

55. Allegro

56. Allegretto

57. Moderato

58. Allegretto

59. Adagietto

60. With spirit

61. Allegretto

62.   Andante con moto

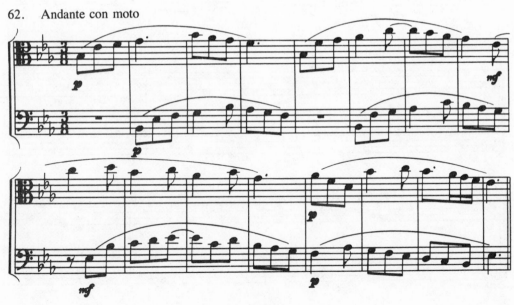

63. Spiritoso

64. Lebhaft und kräftig

65. Lento

66. Andantino

237

67. Lento

68. Andante

69. Andante con moto

70. Deciso

71. Lento

72. Langsam

73. Moderately fast

DUETS *Section IV*

74.   Allegro giocoso

75.   Etwas langsam

76. Allegretto

77. Allegro

78. Adagio non tanto

79. Andante

80. Con fuoco

81. Andante

82. Andante

83. Vivo

84. Ziemlich langsam

85. Adagietto

*Appoggiatura; see Glossary.

86. Nicht zu schnell

87. Andante con moto

88. Moderato

89. Andante espressivo

90. Molto lento

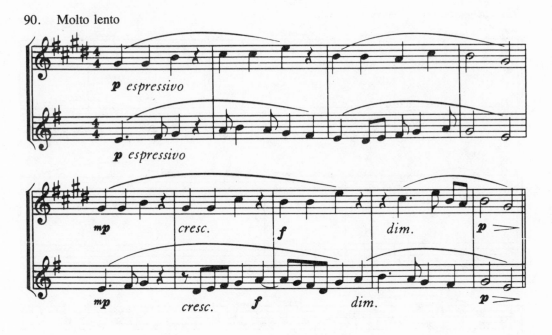

91. Moderato

92. Allegretto e marcato

93. March

94. Allegro

95. Ruhig ♩ = 54

CHAPTER FOUR
PLAY AND SING

SECTIONS I, II, III, AND IV ARE TO BE USED WITH SECTIONS I, II, III, AND IV OF ALL OTHER CHAPTERS.

These exercises are designed to provide a preparatory experience in sight singing vocal music with piano accompaniment. The piano will be especially useful to those who have difficulties with intonation.

These little pieces should be played and sung by the same person. Therefore the piano parts have been kept at a minimum level of difficulty. The emphasis is upon the melodic line and its relationship to the accompaniment. Students with little pianistic ability may use the duets of Chapter Three as additional easy play and sing exercises.

The skill acquired through the study of this chapter will allow the student to become familiar with some of the richest treasures in the musical literature. He should continue to explore all manner of music, instrumental as well as vocal.

PLAY AND SING *Section I*

11. Andante

12. Andante

13. Allegretto

14. Andante

15. Allegro

16. Moderato

17. Allegretto

18a. Andante (Maggiore)

18b. Andante (Minore)

19a. Andantino (Maggiore)

19b. Andantino (Minore)

PLAY AND SING *Section II*

20. Moderato

24. Allegretto

25. Allegro

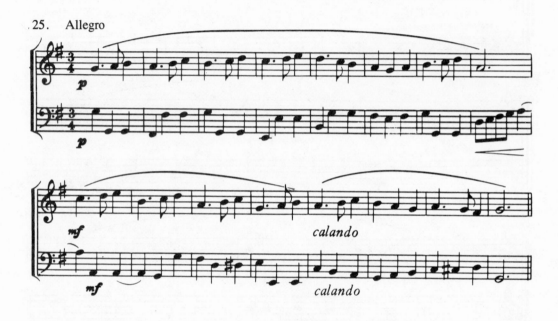

calando

calando

26. Andante

27. Allegretto

28. Andante

29. Lento

30. Andante

31. Moderato

32. Allegro

33. Allegretto

34. Lento

35. Allegretto

36. Adagio

37. Andante

38. Andante

42.   Allegro

43.   Moderato

44. Modéré

45. Moderato

46. Andantino

47. Moderato

sempre staccato

48. Langsam

49. Andante

50. Adagio

51. Moderato

52. Allegro assai

53. Andante cantabile

54. Allegretto

55. Lento

56. Andantino

57. Andante con moto

58. Allegretto grazioso

59. Largo

60. Etwas bewegt

61. Pastorale

62. Allegretto

63. Mässig und zart

64. Andantino

65. Pas trop lent

66. Langsam

* *Appoggiatura; see Glossary.*

67. Slowly

68.   Adagio

69.   Berceuse

70. Andante maestoso

71. Mässig und ausdrucksvoll

72. Andante cantabile

73. Allegretto

74. Recitativo

* *Appoggiatura; see Glossary.*

75.   Moderato

76. Innig

77. Andante sostenuto

78. Un poco sostenuto

79.   Mit Empfindung

80. Tempo di valzer

81. Pastorale

82. Vivo

83. Andante con moto

84. Ziemlich langsam

85. Andantino con grazia

86. Slowly

87. Con calore

88. Allegro con brio

89. Largo

90. Lento

91. Con calma

92. Tenderly

93. Ziemlich langsam

94. Teneramente

95. Energetic, not too fast

96. Slowly

97.   Slow and expressive

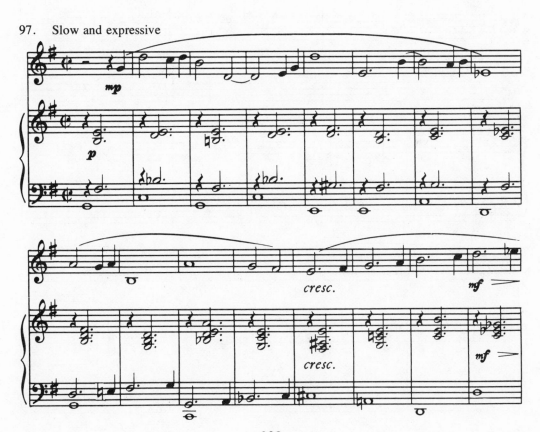

98. Jazz waltz

99. Andantino

100. Doux et espressif

101. Molto sostenuto

102. Modéré

103. Lentement

104. Ruhig ♩ = 72

CHAPTER FIVE
IMPROVISATION STUDIES
SECTIONS I, II, III, AND IV ARE TO BE USED WITH SECTIONS I, II, III, AND IV OF ALL OTHER CHAPTERS.

These exercises are intended to help the student explore the relationships of melody, harmony, and rhythm. A group of harmonic and rhythmic patterns is presented; the student must improvise a melodic line. In so doing he must of necessity give attention to the manner in which the melodic line, the underlying harmony, and the rhythmic structure combine to make up the musical whole. At the same time he must think in terms of a complete musical phrase. His creative impulse will be stimulated.

Before attempting an improvisation, the student should analyze and memorize the harmonic pattern. Next he should study the first of the rhythmic patterns listed under each chord sequence. Then he should improvise a melody using the given rhythmic pattern while accompanying himself with the harmonic sequences. He may begin by modeling his improvisation upon the illustrative examples which open each section. The melody need not be limited to chord tones; on the contrary, it can be considerably enhanced by the use of nonharmonic tones. When the student has completed the exercises which are given, he himself should invent rhythmic and harmonic patterns for further improvisation.

Since these are improvisation studies, no tempo or dynamic markings are given. The student should determine the tempo (fast? slow? medium?) and the dynamic level (loud? soft? crescendo?) before attempting each exercise.

1.

a

Example

b

c

d

e

Example

7.

11.

12.

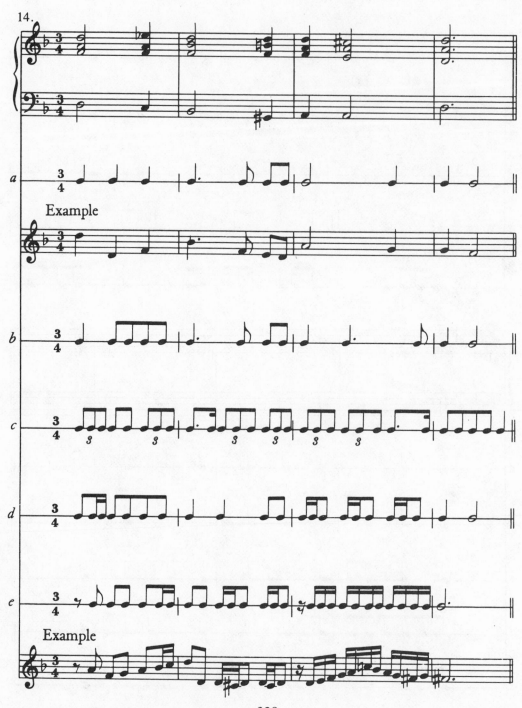

SUPPLEMENTARY EXERCISES

These drills are designed to focus upon various technical problems. Part I is concerned principally with problems of intonation and the development of the sense of key. Part II concentrates upon problems involving chromaticism. Both parts also contain rhythmic patterns arranged in order of increasing complexity. We suggest that the student first learn an exercise slowly and accurately, then increase the speed as much as possible.

SUPPLEMENTARY EXERCISES *Part I*
EXERCISES FOR USE WITH SECTIONS I AND II

9.

Exercises 10–13 are designed to show similarities and differences between the major and minor modes.

10a.   Major

10b.   Melodic minor

10c.   Natural minor

10d.   Harmonic minor

11a.   Major

11b.   Melodic minor

11c.   Natural minor

11d.   Harmonic minor

SUPPLEMENTARY EXERCISES *Part II*

EXERCISES FOR USE WITH SECTIONS III AND IV

81. Ionian mode (major scale)

82. Aeolian mode (natural minor scale)

83. Harmonic minor scale

84. Melodic minor scale

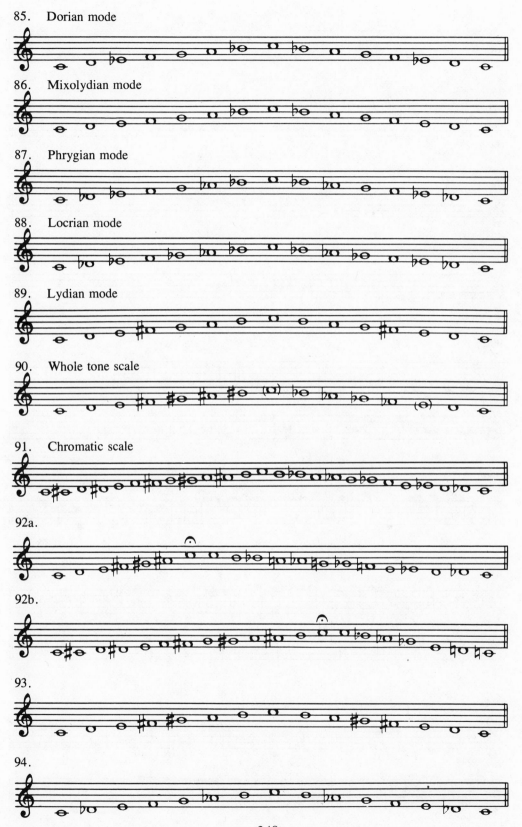

85. Dorian mode

86. Mixolydian mode

87. Phrygian mode

88. Locrian mode

89. Lydian mode

90. Whole tone scale

91. Chromatic scale

92a.

92b.

93.

94.

95.

116.

117.

118.

119.

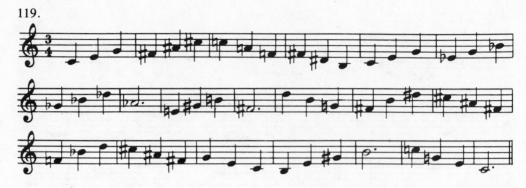

120.

121.

122.

123.

124.

125.

126.

127.

128.

129.

130.

131.

132. Rhythmic Variations on a Tone Row

a. Moderato

b. Andante

c. Allegro

d. Presto

APPENDIX I: GLOSSARY OF MUSICAL TERMS

ALL TERMS ARE ITALIAN UNLESS OTHERWISE NOTED. ABBREVIATIONS ARE GIVEN IN PARENTHESES.

Accelerando (accel.), gradually getting faster

Adagietto, somewhat faster than adagio

Adagio, slow (slower than andante, faster than largo)

Agitato, agitated

Al fine, to the end

Alla, to the, at the, in the style of

Allargando, getting slower (crescendo often implied)

Allegretto, moderately fast (slower than allegro, faster than andante)

Allegro, fast, cheerful

All'ottava (8va), at the octave

Andante, moderately slow (slower than allegretto, faster than adagio)

Andantino, in modern usage, somewhat faster than andante; in older usage, somewhat slower than andante

Anima, spirit

Animato, animated, spirited

Animé, Fr., animated, spirited

Appassionato, impassioned, intense

Appoggiatura, a melodic ornament; of the many types there are two main classifications: the *accented (long) appoggiatura* and the *short appoggiatura* (grace note). The first, written as a small note, is accented and borrows time value from the note it precedes. The second is usually written as a small eighth or sixteenth note with a slanting stroke through the flag and stem. It is executed quickly, so that the accent falls on the melody note it precedes.

Arietta, a small aria

Assai, very

Assez, Fr., fairly

A tempo, in the original speed

Attacca, attack or begin what follows without pause

Ausdrucksvoll, Ger., expressive

Avec, Fr., with

Ballando, dancing

Ben, well, very

Berceuse, Fr., lullaby

Bewegt, Ger., rather fast, agitated

358

Breit, Ger., broad, stately
Brillante, brilliant, sparkling
Brio, sprightliness, spirit

Calando, decreasing in both dynamics and tempo
Calma, Calmo, calm, tranquil
Calore, warmth, passion
Cantabile, in a singing or vocal style
Comodo, at a leisurely, convenient pace
Con, with
Crescendo (cresc.), increasing in volume of sound

Da capo (D. C.), from the beginning
Da capo al fine, repeat from the beginning to the end; that is, to the place where *fine* is written
Dal segno al fine, repeat from the sign to the end; that is, to the place where *fine* is written
Deciso, decisive, bold
Decrescendo (decresc.), decreasing in volume of sound
Del, of the
Détaché, Fr., detached
Di, of
Diminuendo (dim.), decreasing in volume of sound
Dolce, sweet (*soft* is also implied)
Doux, Fr., sweet (*soft* is also implied)
Doucement, Fr., sweet (*soft* is also implied)

E, ed, and
Eco, echo
Einfach, Ger., simple
Empfindung, Ger., expression
En allant, Fr., moving, flowing
Energico, energetic
Espressione, expression
Et, Fr., and
Espressivo (espr.), expressive
Etwas, Ger., somewhat
Expressif, Fr., expressive

Fine, end
Fliessend, Ger., flowing
Force, Fr., strength, force
Forte (f), loud
Fortissimo (ff), very loud
Frisch, Ger., brisk, lively
Fröhlich, Ger., joyous, gay
Fuoco, fire

Gai, Fr., gay
Gaio, gay
Galop, Fr., a lively round-dance in duple meter
Gavotte, Fr., a French dance generally in common time, strongly accented, beginning on the third beat
Gedehnt, Ger., extended, sustained

359

Gigue, Fr., jig, a very fast dance of English origin in triple or sextuple meter
Giocoso, playful
Gioviale, jovial
Giusto, exact
Gracieux, Fr., graceful
Grave, very slow, solemn (generally indicates the slowest tempo)
Grazia, grace
Grazioso, graceful

Il più, the most
Im Zeitmass, Ger., in the original speed
Innig, Ger., heartfelt, ardent
Innocente, unaffected, artless

Kraft, Ger., strength
Kräftig, Ger., strong, robust

La, It. and Fr., the
Ländler, Ger., a country dance in triple meter
Langsam, Ger., slow
Larghetto, not as slow as largo
Largo, slow, broad
Lebhaft, Ger., lively, animated
Legato, to be performed with no interruption between tones; in a smooth and connected manner
Léger, Fr., light
Leggiero (also *Leggero*), light, delicate
Lent, Fr., slow
Lentement, Fr., slowly
Lento, slow; not as slow as adagio
L'istesso tempo, in the same tempo as the previous section
Lunatico, performed in the spirit of lunacy

Ma, but
Maestoso, majestic, dignified
Maggiore, major (referring to mode)
Mais, Fr., but
Marcato, marked, with emphasis
Marcia, march
Marziale, martial
Mässig, Ger., moderate
Mazurka, Polish national dance in triple meter
Meno, less
Mesto, sad, mournful
Mezzo forte (mf), moderately loud
Mezzo piano (mp), moderately soft
Minore, minor (referring to mode)
Minuetto, minuet (moderately slow dance in triple meter)
Misterioso, mysterious
Mit, Ger., with
Moderato, moderate (slower than allegro, faster than andante)
Modéré, Fr., moderate (slower than allegro, faster than andante)

Möglich, Ger., possible
Molto, much very
Morendo, dying away
Mosso, in motion (*più mosso*, faster; *meno mosso*, slower)
Moto, motion
Mouvement, Fr., motion, tempo, movement
Munter, Ger., lively

Nicht, Ger., not
Niente, nothing
Non, not

Ongarese, Hungarian

Pas, Fr., not
Pastorale, pastoral
Perdendosi, gradually fading away
Pesante, heavy, ponderous
Peu, Fr., little
Piacevole, pleasant, graceful
Piano (p), soft
Pianissimo (pp), very soft
Più, more
Plus, Fr., more
Poco, little
Poco a poco, little by little, gradually
Pomposo, pompous
Possibile, possible
Pressez, Fr., press forward
Presto, very fast (faster than allegro)

Quasi, almost, nearly

Rallentando (rall.), gradually growing slower
Rasch, Ger., fast
Recitativo, sung in a declamatory manner
Retenu, Fr., held back
Rigore, strictness
Risoluto, firm, resolute
Ritardando (rit.), gradually growing slower
Ritenuto (riten.), held back
Ritmico, rhythmically
Rubato, literally, stolen; the term indicates freedom and flexibility of tempo so that the requirements of musical expression can be met
Ruhig, Ger., calm, tranquil

Saltarello, a lively dance of Italian origin, often in $\frac{9}{8}$
Scherzando, light, playful
Scherzo, a fast piece in triple meter
Scherzoso, jesting, playful
Schnell, Ger., fast
Seconda, second

Sehr, Ger., very
Semplice, simple, unaffected
Sempre, always
Sentimentale, It. and Fr., with sentiment
Sforzando (sf, sfz), with force, accented
Siciliano, a moderately slow dance of pastoral character in $\frac{12}{8}$ or $\frac{6}{8}$ time
Simile, alike, in like manner
So, Ger., as
Sostenuto, sustained
Sotto voce, softly, with subdued voice
Spirito, spirit
Spiritoso, with spirit, animated
Staccato, detached
Stark, Ger., strong, vigorous
Stringendo, pressing forward
Subito (sub.), suddenly

Tanto, so much
Tarantella, a lively dance of Italian origin, usually in $\frac{6}{8}$
Tempo, time; refers to rate of motion
Tempo primo (Tempo I), in the original speed
Teneramente, tenderly, delicately
Tranquillo, tranquil
Très, Fr., very
Triste, It. and Fr., sad
Trop, Fr., too much, too
Troppo, too much, too

Un, It. and Fr., a
Und, Ger., and

Valse, Fr., waltz
Valzer, waltz
Vif, Fr., lively
Vite, Fr., quickly
Vivace, lively, quick
Vivo, lively, animated
Volta, turn or time

Walzer, Ger., waltz
Wie, Ger., as

Zart, Ger., tender, soft
Zeitmass, Ger., tempo
Ziemlich, Ger., somewhat, rather
Zu, Ger., too, to, by
Zuvor, Ger., previously
Zurückhalten, Ger., to hold back, to retard

Appendix II: Some Frequently Used Musical Signs

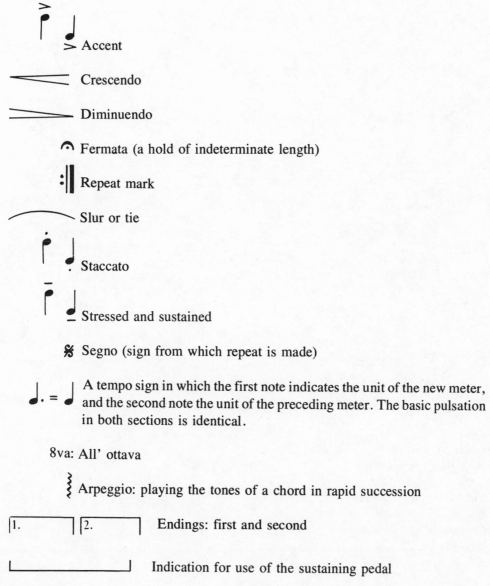

> Accent

Crescendo

Diminuendo

Fermata (a hold of indeterminate length)

Repeat mark

Slur or tie

Staccato

Stressed and sustained

Segno (sign from which repeat is made)

♩. = ♩ A tempo sign in which the first note indicates the unit of the new meter, and the second note the unit of the preceding meter. The basic pulsation in both sections is identical.

8va: All' ottava

Arpeggio: playing the tones of a chord in rapid succession

1.   2.   Endings: first and second

Indication for use of the sustaining pedal

363